NATURAL GAS ENERGY

PUTTING GAS TO WORK

JESSIE ALKIRE

Consulting Editor, Diane Craig, M.A./Reading Specialist

Super Sandcastle

An Imprint of Abdo Publishing
abdopublishing.com

abdopublishing.com

Published by Abdo Publishing, a division of ABDO, PO Box 398166, Minneapolis, Minnesota 55439. Copyright © 2019 by Abdo Consulting Group, Inc. International copyrights reserved in all countries. No part of this book may be reproduced in any form without written permission from the publisher. Super SandCastle™ is a trademark and logo of Abdo Publishing.

Printed in the United States of America, North Mankato, Minnesota

052018
092018

Design and Production: Mighty Media, Inc.
Editor: Megan Borgert-Spaniol
Cover Photographs: Shutterstock; Wikimedia Commons
Interior Photographs: iStockphoto; LarryGrim/Wikimedia Commons; Mighty Media, Inc.; Shutterstock; Wikimedia Commons

Library of Congress Control Number: 2017961851

Publisher's Cataloging-in-Publication Data
Names: Alkire, Jessie, author.
Title: Natural gas energy: Putting gas to work / by Jessie Alkire.
Other titles: Putting gas to work
Description: Minneapolis, Minnesota : Abdo Publishing, 2019. | Series: Earth's energy innovations
Identifiers: ISBN 9781532115721 (lib.bdg.) | ISBN 9781532156441 (ebook)
Subjects: LCSH: Natural gas as fuel--Juvenile literature. | Power resources--Juvenile literature. | Energy development--Juvenile literature. | Energy conversion--Juvenile literature.
Classification: DDC 553.285--dc23

Super SandCastle™ books are created by a team of professional educators, reading specialists, and content developers around five essential components—phonemic awareness, phonics, vocabulary, text comprehension, and fluency—to assist young readers as they develop reading skills and strategies and increase their general knowledge. All books are written, reviewed, and leveled for guided reading, early reading intervention, and Accelerated Reader™ programs for use in shared, guided, and independent reading and writing activities to support a balanced approach to literacy instruction.

CONTENTS

WHAT IS NATURAL GAS ENERGY?

Natural gas drilling rig

Natural gas energy is energy created by burning natural gas. Natural gas is a **fossil fuel**. It forms from the remains of plants and animals. The remains get buried deep underground. They give off gas as they break down.

People drill into Earth for natural gas. They use the gas for heat, power, and more!

Heat and pressure turn the remains of plants and animals into natural gas, coal, and oil. This process takes millions of years!

OCEAN 300 TO 400 MILLION YEARS AGO

OCEAN 50 TO 100 MILLION YEARS AGO

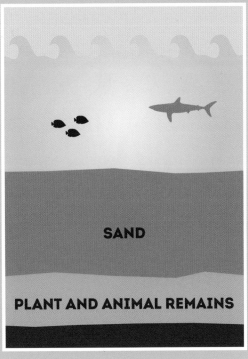

SAND

PLANT AND ANIMAL REMAINS

OCEAN TODAY

OFFSHORE NATURAL GAS DRILLING RIG

ROCK

NATURAL GAS   COAL   OIL

ENERGY TIMELINE

500 BCE

People in China **transport** natural gas through bamboo pipelines.

1785 CE

Britain uses natural gas made from coal to light homes and streets.

1816

The first US gas streetlight is used in Baltimore, Maryland.

Discover how natural gas energy has changed over time!

1855

Robert Bunsen invents
the Bunsen burner.

1900s

Many pipelines are built.
They **transport** natural
gas across countries.

2016

Natural gas is the largest
source of US electricity.

HEAT AND LIGHT

Natural gas was first used around 500 BCE. People in China burned it to boil seawater. They **transported** the gas through bamboo pipelines.

In 1785, natural gas made from coal lit homes and streets in Britain. This type of gas lighting soon spread to other cities. In 1816, it lit streetlights in Baltimore, Maryland.

First US gas streetlight in Baltimore

In the 1800s, cities hired lamplighters to light gas streetlights at night. Lamplighters are less common today.

BURNING UP

Bunsen burner

The first US natural gas well was drilled in 1821. It was in Fredonia, New York. The first US natural gas company later formed there.

In 1855, Robert Bunsen invented the Bunsen burner. It used natural gas to produce a flame for heating.

In the 1900s, many pipelines were built. They **transported** natural gas.

ROBERT BUNSEN

BORN: March 30, 1811, Göttingen, Germany

DIED: August 16, 1899, Heidelberg, Germany

Robert Bunsen was a German scientist. He made many discoveries and inventions. One invention was the Bunsen burner. It was based on models by other scientists. The burner mixed air and natural gas. It could then be lit to create a flame. Bunsen burners are still used today!

CLEANER ENERGY

Natural gas supplies much of the world's energy. Gas pipelines run across countries. The gas is used to heat and power buildings.

Natural gas burns cleaner than other **fossil fuels**. But it still produces **greenhouse gases**. Drilling for gas can also cause gas leaks. Leaks can start fires and harm wildlife.

Burning natural gas

Some natural gas wells are drilled offshore in the ocean. These wells often pump both oil and gas.

HEAT, POWER, AND FUEL

Natural gas energy is used for heating. It provides heat in homes, businesses, and factories. It is also used for cooking.

Natural gas is burned at power plants. The heat energy is used to create electricity.

Natural gas vehicle

Some **vehicles** run on natural gas. They produce less pollution than **gasoline** vehicles.

Many stoves and ovens are fueled by natural gas. They burn the gas to produce heat for cooking.

DRILLING WELLS

Most natural gas is found deep underground. Scientists look for rocks that trap natural gas. Workers drill natural gas wells into the rocks. Gas is pumped through the wells.

Fracking site

Some wells use a method called fracking. Fracking pumps water and sand into rock. Cracks form in the rock. This lets gas flow more freely.

Fracking can cause pollution. It has also caused small earthquakes. This is when the ground shakes or trembles.

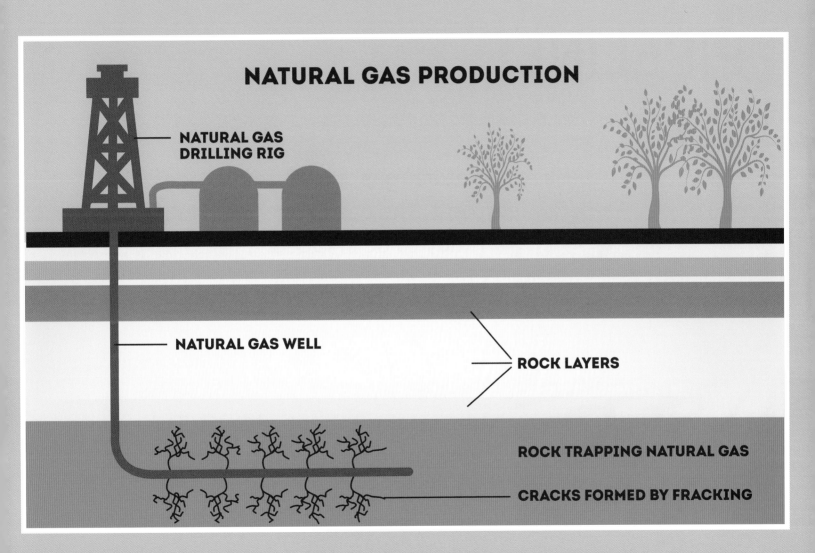

NATURAL GAS PRODUCTION

NATURAL GAS
DRILLING RIG

NATURAL GAS WELL

ROCK LAYERS

ROCK TRAPPING NATURAL GAS

CRACKS FORMED BY FRACKING

PIPELINES

Natural gas is sent to a processing plant. The gas is purified. Then it is ready to be shipped.

Natural gas is usually shipped through pipelines. Gas can travel thousands of miles in these pipes! Smaller pipes carry the gas into homes and other buildings. The gas is ready to be used!

Natural gas processing plant

Natural gas pipeline construction

TOP FOSSIL FUEL

Natural gas is an important energy **resource**. It was the largest source of US electricity in 2016.
But natural gas is not renewable. And drilling for gas can harm the **environment**.

Operator at natural gas plant

Scientists look for new natural gas sources. They also explore new methods of reaching the gas. Natural gas may be the **fossil fuel** of the **future**!

Texas is a top US producer and consumer of natural gas.

MORE ABOUT NATURAL GAS ENERGY

Do you want to tell others about natural gas energy? Here are some fun facts to share!

ANCIENT PEOPLE discovered natural gas when it came up through cracks in the ground. **Lightning** would set the gas on fire!

THE US GAS PIPELINE SYSTEM could reach to the moon and back twice if the pipes were laid end to end!

CHEMICALS are added to natural gas to make it smell like rotten eggs. This lets people know if there is a gas leak!

TEST YOUR KNOWLEDGE

1. In what year did Robert Bunsen invent the Bunsen burner?

2. Natural gas can power some **vehicles**. **TRUE OR FALSE?**

3. What method uses water and sand to form cracks in rock?

THINK ABOUT IT!

Have you seen the blue flame of a gas stove? This is natural gas energy at work!

ANSWERS: 1. 1855 2. True 3. Fracking

GLOSSARY

environment – nature and everything in it, such as the land, sea, and air.

fossil fuel – a fuel formed from the remains of plants or animals. Coal, oil, and natural gas are fossil fuels.

future – the time that hasn't happened yet.

gasoline – a liquid that can burn that is used to power engines.

greenhouse gas – a gas, such as carbon dioxide, that traps heat in Earth's atmosphere.

lightning – a flash of light caused by electricity in the air.

resource – something that is usable or valuable.

transport – to move something from one place to another.

vehicle – something used to carry persons or large objects. Examples include cars, trucks, and buses.